Lost in the Dance

DEREK PICKETT
Poetry, Visions & Movement

LOST IN THE DANCE
Copyright © 2020, Derek Pickett
All Rights and International Rights Reserved.

Names, characters, places, and incidents are the product of the author's imagination. While some historical figures and places are real, all have been used ficticiously. Any resemblance to actual locales, events or persons, living or dead, is entirely coincidental.

No part of this book or any portion thereof may be reproduced, distributed, or transmitted in any form or by any means, including photocopying, recording, or other electronic or mechanical methods, nor may it be stored in a retrieval system, transmitted or otherwise copied for public or private use, without the prior written permission of the publisher, except in the case of "fair use" of brief quotations embodied in critical reviews and certain other noncommercial uses permitted by copyright law.

For permission requests, contact the author at: infoLITD@yahoo.com

All photography is copyrighted by Derek Pickett (except as noted) and may not be reproduced by any means, electronic or otherwise, without first obtaining the written permission of Derek Pickett.

First Printing, 2020
ISBN-978-0-578-81318-9

Cover and page design by www.MarkGelotte.com

DEDICATION

This book is dedicated to my children John-Paul and Gabrielle Conway, you are my inspiration. May the world shine its love and light your way. Thank you to my dear friends and editors: Lynn Colwell, Lynn Popkowski, Judith Watson, Justine Gaston, Diane Feagin and Kelly Norton. Your energy and enthusiasm brought this project to life.

INTRODUCTION

Derek's love of dance, travel, nature, music and people blend in a beautiful tapestry of life in this collection of poetry. Memories of his years growing up in England dance alongside energetic scenes in the streets of New York, pubs of Ireland and the dance halls of Houston. Poems about nature, spirituality and romance comingle in a melody of oneness, love and harmony. The dance poems that weave throughout the collection carry the overriding theme of connection. To live in a world as imagined and revealed by Derek's poetry is truly a reality to be sought after. Absorb yourself in the joy of the poetry, the joy of travel, backyard retreats, living, loving and, of course, the joy of dance.

— Lynn Colwell

LOST IN THE DANCE

1. Lost in the Dance
3. Silent Town
5. Something I Did Not Know I Was Missing
7. May You
9. Morning Song
11. Homeward Herd

13. It's Friday Night She Wants to Dance
15. New York City
17. Ocean Lady
19. Grace in the Storm
21. The Feeling Sought
23. My Friend the Moon

25. Dancing Houston
27. Dublin
29. We Grew Each Other
31. To Be in Tune
33. Manners Maketh Man
35. Lured by Love

37. Old Dance Hall
39. English Celebration
41. In Your Sweet Arms
43. Safe Harbor
45. Mind, Wine and Music
47. By the Light of the Moon

49. The Joy of Dance
51. Dusty Cumbia
53. Coral Strand
55. The Yard
57. Namaste
59. The Moon in Gemini

60. Derek Pickett

Lost in the dance

Photo courtesy Wild West, Houston

LOST IN THE DANCE

The music breaks in, it inspires the advance,
he can see from her smile she is wanting to dance.
The soft waltz plays, it touches her soul,
as he offers his hand inviting and bold.

Leading her forward, he holds her in place,
as the expectation shines from her face.
She follows with gusto, she's perfect in beat,
with style and with grace, a movable treat.

Led with wisdom, in harmony sublime,
they are proud and secure and completely in time.
Joined together, to the music they dance,
moving as one in a rhythmic romance.

As they move and they sway she is carried away,
lost in the dance and freed from her day.
On a voyage to Venus, to Mars and beyond,
floating on air for the length of a song.

Time to set your spirit free

SILENT TOWN

Downtown our town
all at once a ghost town
No traffic trains no theater shows
streets abandoned cafes closed
just the tumbleweeds rolling down
the silent streets of Houston town

Downtown closed down
stillness darkness all around
don't see a soul don't hear a sound
No sirens horns no fights no scorn
only peace and quiet found
on the silent streets of Houston town

Time to walk reflect find your thoughts
gone the pressure gone the busy bustle crazy fraught
time to set your spirit free
let those pent-up hopes abound
take your time find your feet
walking silent streets of Houston town

The bar is bustling with joy and jokes, relaxing revelry

SOMETHING I DID NOT KNOW I WAS MISSING

The smell of stew and the promise of ale draw us in
the baritone in the corner woos us with renderings of folk tunes and Dylan covers
the bar is bustling with joy and jokes, relaxing revelry—
a bunch of old guys sit with their pints, smiling out kindness—
wisdom and warmth etched in the lines of their faces
Across the room with passion and conviction, fueled by whiskey
the girls from Dublin are singing the chorus of *The Fields of Athenry*
American tourists blend with Europeans and locals—
this is home, we all live here, for tonight at least
Intrigue, interest, dialogue and flirting are mingled in the smoke-free air—
and I become best friends with a stranger for just a couple of hours—
sharing drinks and laughter - a tonic for all that ails the human spirit
I savor the joy of making new acquaintances
and drink in the power of smiles and words offered in jest
We can be judgmental and see all the sin induced by alcohol
but I see comradery and community—
I want to be here and share in this guilty pleasure
I want to lose myself for a long, long while—
in something I did not know I was missing

Relax with peace and inner calm

Beach Still Life by Gabrielle Conway

MAY YOU

May you soar in confidence
yet always remain balanced, kind and humble
be rescued and renewed
if you should falter, fail or stumble.
May you love without limit
and feel the warmth and power of love returned
share your wisdom and your counsel,
and those life lessons through time you've learned.

May you be reliable and ready,
righteous in rebellion, stand resilient in resolve
stay safe in your spirit, be patient and placid,
as your problems you face and solve.
May you be blessed with labors,
which bring you purpose, joy and fascination.
May you dance through life with a graceful kindred spirit,
who's right there with you in every situation.

May you be lucid and learned, and for new knowledge
may you always hunger and thirst
be assured and indomitable,
if others should try to show you their very worst.
May you be absorbed in sonnets, songs and silence,
solitude and sunsets serene.
May you create and collaborate,
be validated, an integral part of any team.

May you let your imagination lead you
to fabulous far off foreign lands,
keep body and soul in tune, feet always firmly planted,
life safe in your own hands.
May you always have perspective
and joy from simple pleasures may you always find,
relax, with peace and inner calm,
float upstream and free your mind.

May you keep your intrigue and your innocence,
releasing that which does not serve you.
May the world shine its light and love your way,
bring delight and dedication to all that you may do.

The ocean breeze flows in fresh and gentle on my face

MORNING SONG

Through the window I hear waves lapping gently in unison
as they grace the silky shore
The ocean breeze flows in fresh and gentle on my face

The cuckoo is heard vaguely calling from the black barn
a mile or so across the rolling fields
as larks nearby are singing their morning song
to celebrate in the fragrant spring air

I hear the sound of the tamale vendor whistling out his arrival
as dogs bark intermittently from neighboring streets
and that special someone lays gently breathing in sleep
warm and tender beside me

Traffic drones some twenty floors below as the city begins to wake
the hazy din promises daylight and bagels coffee and life
The music of the streets calls us to rise and embrace the breaking day

Wading surely and softly through the room

Homeward Herd by Gabrielle Conway

HOMEWARD HERD

They could be heard off in the distance
rumbling quietly in through the trees across the Savannah
calling out with faint trumpets as they traversed the terrain
making their way steadily and surely towards home

They came into view as regal and regimented they enter now
the gentle giants wading surely and softly through the room
the water lilies bow their blooms in humble harmony
to welcome the herd home

She wants to dance

IT'S FRIDAY NIGHT
SHE WANTS TO DANCE

From the gaudy grandeur of gas profits
to a dirty danced-out honky-tonk
she's counting down the busy hours
and hears guitars begin to strum
still a thousand keyboard clicks
till cheap wine is sipped from a cloudy glass
lost in conference lost in a trance
it's Friday night she wants to dance

She shouts a goodbye to the day
co-workers warmly bid goodnight
flying out across the city
thoughts of spinning round the floor
skirt and Louboutins are traded
for wranglers and Luccheses
it's time to leave it all to chance
it's Friday night she wants to dance

The nightmare Houston traffic
seems everybody wants to fight
nothing halts her mission
her voyage to the stars
a hundred partners lay in waiting
with their able hands outstretched
to polka promenade and prance
it's Friday night she wants to dance

Seeking respite from the noise
through loud and crackly speakers
turning slowly into sweethearts
she finds the ointment for life's hurt
country songs of perfect misery
at one now with the music
lost in three-quarter time romance
it's Friday night she wants to dance

My soul is waiting there

NEW YORK CITY

Take me back to New York City
let me walk those busy streets
smell the bagels and hot chestnuts
eat delicious sidewalk treats

Be in the shadows of tall buildings
towering to the sky
with the din of horns and sirens
a throng of voices milling by

Safe in the streets with people
pollution cops and grime
where I can walk and lose myself
and find a New York state of mind

Ride the ferry with the tourists
gaze at the river from my room
see the Ninth Street bridge in all its grandeur
lit up by the moon

Let me walk those city streets
let me hear New Yorkers yell
with the homeless and street vendors
buying junk which they may sell

Let me wander in Times Square
let me amble in the park
drink Guinness at the Slainte bar
at night when it gets dark

Take me back to New York City
my soul is waiting there
so then about my troubles
I truly would not care

Shimmering lapping the waves are calling me

OCEAN LADY

Coastal girl water baby
harbor princess ocean lady
Rolling seas reflect from pretty green eyes
gulls sing out your name
high up in majestic skies
Shells in the sand lead me
to coves cool and shady
shimmering lapping
the waves are calling me
calling me home
to the ocean lady

Grace in the storm

GRACE IN THE STORM

The rains came down and flooded our world
plans and dreams and so much of our lives
lost forever in the swirl.
Then the storm passed and the sun came out
and angels came calling from north and from south.
Houstonians and strangers together they toiled
rebuilding our city with fervor and joy.

They came in their boats from Louisiana
from Mexico, New York and Arizona.
They came and they stayed, they worked and they prayed
rescuing people and clearing the way
distributing food and handing out love
guided and driven by God above.

A metropolis of cultures
helping each other to find a dry place
together we stood, a brotherhood of kindness
in our melting pot of neighborly grace.
Mack gave us shelter from the storm
Howard gave food and Beaver gave all.
Sylvester our Mayor led with purpose and compassion
a true leader in crisis, he helped us stand tall.

The storm it came and tested our grit
questioning our will to overcome and survive.
But this is the city of General Sam Houston
which nothing can ever defeat or divide.
It was rain and weather not right and not wrong
but we'll renew and rebuild, for you know this is Texas
and we're Houston strong.

It lives in grace and gratitude

Sunset Serene by Gabrielle Conway

THE FEELING SOUGHT

We need it so bad that we are driven to ask and implore
to seek it and need it again and again
to banish our fears, provide all that we lack
rekindle our worth and ease our pain.

When we find it, we know it
then we know it's all we need.
We crave the feeling we desire so much to give it
to set that feeling free.

It's in the hug, the smile, the unexpected anonymous gift
the olive branch and humble offering
the words and feelings
which heal the rift.

When we're happy and grateful, sharing our talents and time
when we connect with society
when we find that special someone
it truly feels sublime.

It may be given, it may be found, it can be taught, it can be true
it lives in grace and gratitude
it's there for the young, rich, poor and old
there for me and there for you.

It feels better when given and yet so good when received.
Some seek it for a lifetime
and some find it so simply
just because they believed.

We seek it from family, friends and strangers
from whatever power we perceive above.
It's a purpose, a prize, it's that unseen emotion
that all powerful feeling, that thing called Love.

My friend you were on dark and starless nights

MY FRIEND THE MOON

My friend you were on dark and starless nights,
walking a country lane home with no street lights.
I'd been to the village and had me a skin-full,
drinking and revelry and all things sinful.

Needing my home and my nice warm bed,
but I was out and alone in the night instead.
Gingerly walking among owls and trees,
out there in nature with the birds and the bees.

I imagined strangers who'd give me a fright,
foxes and critters and things of the night.
But there was no need to fret nor cause for fear,
for my dear friend the moon was always quite near.

Selene shone her light and all was well,
she conquered the darkness and broke its spell,
there with me always whether crescent or full,
romantic and silver a magnificent jewel.

You honored the tides for night and for day,
loyal light in the darkness to guide our way.
Flying through cloud or sailing for home,
through all those nights, I was never alone.

You bring us comfort, shine full on our path,
you watch as we dance and cry and live and laugh.
You beam down upon us and protect us in sleep,
bring us safely to morning for Eos to keep.

It's all about the music, it's all about the dance

Photos courtesy of West West, Houston and Westwind Club, Houston

DANCING HOUSTON

Dancing at a honky-tonk is where I wanna be,
for a two-step or a polka, cuz dancing sets me free.
And I love to step to rhythm, I love to hit the beat,
just play some country music to get me on my feet.

And if it's country music, that brings you out to dance,
then get yourself to Houston, if you ever get the chance.
Cuz in amongst the hospitals, and pipelines of gas n' oil,
there's a mess of clubs and cafes and a buffet of dance halls.

And in Houston there is dancing of every different kind,
tejano, swing and cha cha, even ballroom you will find.
From polka to merengue, salsa, jive and waltz,
zydeco and west coast, Texas two-step, but of course.

Thursday nights at Whiskey River, Sundays at Wild West,
Saturday nights at Stampede, their dance floor is the best.
So if you're out at Eddie's, Goodnight Charlie's or Westwind,
catch me on the dance floor and I'll take you for a spin.

And there is no time for chatting and it's not about romance,
It's all about the music, it's all about the dance.
So don your boots and get to Houston, get here right away,
join us in the dancing capital of the USA.

Walking down O'Connell, across the Liffey, customs house on the right

DUBLIN

Fine and lovely is this land, it's gorgeous so it is,
a trendy busy city that dances to a jig.
Teeming bars, Bulmers, Guinness, Murphy's, belting out the Pogues,
brimmed with ladies, laughter, yelling, jostling, gentlemen and rogues.

The town folk on the streets, celebrating life and Friday fervor,
talking Yeats and Heaney, in a buzz of noisy murmurs.
Walking down O'Connell, across the Liffey, customs house on the right,
onto Grafton, alive with buskers, singing anthems to the night.

Statues of your heroes hold the spirit of the town,
they cry out poems to enthrall, impressing all who gather round.
Kate O'Brien, Oscar Wilde, they travelled near and far,
Molly sings of that which gratifies, Lynott sings of whiskey in the jar.

And the Irish they are charming, joyous and sincere,
they flow like the Shannon, they're as wholesome as their beer.
That soft sense of humor, makes me feel I am at home,
I'll recall these kind and cultured folk, wherever I may roam.

We grew each other

WE GREW EACH OTHER

We grew each other,
we changed the view.
In warmth and intimacy, we found the ocean,
an idyllic world of tranquil blue.

But not besotted nor identity lost,
not settling for security at any cost.
Nowhere to go then, the drama ensued,
the wheel was bent and could not be reused.

But it's ok to lose though it's hard to move on,
we need fascination, to sing our own song.
For life is short and we need to live large,
we must feed our own soul and remain in charge.

And we learn from each other along the way,
from strangers and friends, what they do and they say.
We share our wisdom, our joy and our grace,
and when the moment is right we'll find our safe place.

Then we'll be vulnerable and open to all,
our passion and love, our body and soul.
We'll find our mate, our partner in crime,
the world will be bright and the words will rhyme.

Created to be in tune

TO BE IN TUNE

We are an orchestra of humanity,
capable of producing soft sonatas,
soaring symphonies and simple songs,
to celebrate and rejoice in our oneness.
We are a multitude of unique sounds.
Our instruments come in different colors
in many shapes and sizes,
designed and constructed in different ways.
All part of a master arrangement,
created for music,
created to be in tune.

And we want to march to the beat of our own drum.
But how might it be if we get on beat
and dance with our fellow musicians?
We may find life's rhythm,
following the divine conductor,
who dwells deep within our heart,
and silence the one who plays only to our ego.
What magnificent music we may make together,
sounds of joy, hope and understanding.
Our spirits in unison, our hearts in harmony,
love played with every note.
Created to be in tune.

Those gifts you gave us, which enriched and guided us for the rest of our lives.

MANNERS MAKETH MAN

Galant, gregarious, soft and kind,
a more affable and amenable person
you could not ever wish to find.

Soft and gentle kiss on the lips,
every time you arrived and when you departed.
Running around to open the car door,
the joy of honoring your lady, was what you imparted.

You were always honest and never crass and never crude,
to desire her company and favor, to offer humor and warmth,
but never to dishonor and never to intrude.

A working man with impeccable presence and powerful prévenance.
A strong sense of pride and strong work ethic
our grateful inheritance.

Cutting fresh flowers when we visited back home
with our girlfriends and wives.
Those gifts you gave us, which enriched and guided us
for the rest of our lives.

It was you who taught me to appreciate, to learn and to understand,
that respect, honesty and chivalry are essential,
but mostly manners maketh man.

A special secret silent world

The Lures by Gabrielle Conway

LURED BY LOVE

Lure me to your ocean world
hidden far far below.
A special secret silent world
where no one ever goes.

Let us be lovingly lured
and lured let us be by love.
Far away from man's transgressions
and all his mayhem up above.

Lure me to your soft white sands
where all the fish are stars.
Lure me to your paradise
or to wherever that you are.

This is where the dancers come to lose themselves

Photo courtesy of Wild West, Houston

OLD DANCE HALL

Sparkly saddles and dusty wagon wheels
watch the dancers from above.
The floor is old and creaky, the place needs some renewal,
but it rings with music, laughter and love.

Here the patrons are abundant, they bring the place alive,
they are adept and present, loyal and loud.
They two-step round the floor, a mix of demographics,
making up the crowd.

There are non-dancing characters who watch, drink and chat,
while propping up the bar.
There are experts and teachers, and many more out there
who like to think that they are.

Grey-haired grandpas and merry millennials
who step in time to the beat,
and those whose twists and turns bear no rhythmic relation
to their flat and rather docile feet.

Emily and Amber smiling from the bar, they don't miss a beat,
they spoil their dancing patrons, with all kinds of refreshing treats.
While Giovanna and Cisco are serving us hot fajitas,
ellos son amables, amigables y su comida es rica y deliciosa.

This is where the dancers come to lose themselves
in music, motion and rhythmic space,
to celebrate and practice, mingle and connect,
and dance some life into this fine old place.

The sun is shining brightly down upon the regal kingdom

ENGLISH CELEBRATION

The sun is shining brightly down upon the regal kingdom,
this fine land is proud and powerful yet.
Ancient bridges and towers stand strong,
their endurance and wisdom chiming loudly out over the lands
where the sun would never set.

I wander no longer lonely as Wordsworth's cloud,
but rejoice, now in the company of my fellow man,
fine history and dreams of what may be,
while tulips and daffodils bellow out spring's mirthful celebration
like a glorious rolling sea.

The people dash every which way,
urgent in the city's hustle and bustle,
a mélange of buses and taxis and tasks to be achieved,
they stop on the Strand now to boldly kiss and revel in their freedom,
their passions aflame for all the world to see.

I could walk forever by the winding river,
feasting on springtime's perfumed glory,
proudly admiring the nation's historic fortitude.
I find my home now in a young lady's beautiful smile
and a young man's confident dialogue.
I have been renewed with pride and joy and gratitude.

I escape from the world, to your love and your charm

IN YOUR SWEET ARMS

You give me shelter, you give me peace,
you soothe the hurt and cause it to cease.
You quell my stress, you make me calm,
I am loved and protected, in your sweet arms.

Finding comfort and refuge, a home from home,
no longer lost, no longer to roam.
Finding warmth and solace, I am safe from harm,
finding quiet forgiveness, in your sweet arms.

I am lost in your paradise, I am born again,
no longer vulnerable, with no fear and no pain.
I escape from the world, to your love and your charm,
I surrender to you, in your sweet arms.

I am your safe harbor

SAFE HARBOR

There is no preconception
no illusion no pretense
no need for prosecution or defense
the answers do not have to make any sense
I am your safe harbor

And you are the owner and the keeper of your space
not everything will have explanation or find its perfect place
sometimes things are gone
and they will leave no trace
I am your safe harbor

I may be the elixir to nurse your hurt
and heal your heart until it mends
I may be your sacred silent Zen
your joyous grateful Amen
and you may call on me again and again
I am your safe harbor

And there are hopeful strands of light
which from your darkness I may glean
draw back life's shutters so that your essence may be seen
shine on your world until it sparkles and it gleams
be your precious amulet so you may sleep and find your dreams
I am your safe harbor

The kind call of distraction is realized

MIND, WINE AND MUSIC

I pick up the glass of red wine and take a sip,
a joyous gift for lips and palate.
My mind is traveling at a thousand miles an hour.
Why did this happen? Why me? What do I do now?
And what if there's more to come?
So begins the long journey to rationalization.

Then I'm aware of the music, and I allow it to flow in.
Pulsing bass and rolling sax wash over me,
sweet rhythms to soothe and calm and carry me away
on a sojourn of respite.
Fueled by the Cabernet, solace and peace are found in the music
a moment of forgiveness, a short refrain.

But I have to resolve this, shouts back the ever-demanding mind
and smashes through the musical haze.
Reproach and questions come flooding back
pounding me like angry waves on the sand.
I reach for the wine in retaliation and switch to sweet soul music
the type I like most at this hour.

Warm strings and cool brass accompany rich voices
and blend with a backbeat of percussion and bluesy guitars.
And as Lizz and Rhiannon softly serenade me
I start to dance it out of my head.
Finally, the mind relents, thoughts are muted
as pleasure is discovered in the moment.
The kind call of distraction is realized
in the fusion of music and wine
bringing relaxation, calm and treasured rest.

In your majestic fullness we are never alone

BY THE LIGHT OF THE MOON

Nature sits patient as you wane for planting
crescent light on the land the cycle is starting
You wax for the farmer at work in the field
shine down your harvest his crops for to yield

Fruit will flourish the land shall provide
a divine bouquet in radiance to imbibe
Clouds drift away the quarter does loom
you cast your shadows for darkness comes soon

Soft words are spoken serene and bright
revelations may be realized by your silvery light
Savor the tannins with intrigue and delight
revel in the mystique and the glow of the night

You guide our path as we make our way home
in your majestic fullness we are never alone
When the world is dark and life is forbidding
you energize the soul and shine on our being

Immerse in the thrill, the abandon and the joy of dance

Photo Courtesy SSQQ Dance Studio

THE JOY OF DANCE

They watch from the rail they admire from the bars
stars of the dance floor like Venus and Mars

We move in harmony and glide in time
a paragon of rhythm, a joyous rhyme

We savor the moment of movement divine
consumed by sound, luscious fruit on the vine

Warmth and friendship, camaraderie and community
embraced in song and signature unity

We relax the soul and free the mind
rejuvenation and renewal in good music we find

We pose the question, we take a chance
and immerse in the thrill, the abandon and the joy of dance

Gone from hurricane, humid Houston to stately, sensual Southern England

DUSTY CUMBIA

I'm walking the quiet, abandoned tunnels under Houston town.
All those businesses closed and silent,
it makes me sad it brings me down.
Then music is heard, some signs of life and light are found,
a subterranean party, maybe a little fiesta deep underground.

But the music's a mix and my ears are confused
and can't determine the rhythm.
Sounds like pop and cumbia,
but the beat is off and the melodies are hidden.
As I get closer, the cumbia is pumping,
I see *chicas bonitas* serving coffee n' tacos.
I order chicken fajita with nopales and tomatoes.

The food is rica, I relax and my hips start to sway to the cumbia beat,
I want so much to dance.
I think about Mexico, *mercados, mujeres guapas*, tequila and romance.
As I munch on my tacos, lost in Mexico, walking along,
the music changes to something old and familiar,
it sounds like a famous old sixties song.

Yeah, I hear it now from that fine and fabulous lady:
I only wanna be with you.
That sweet English voice, singing warm and bluesy and true.
I remember her singing on Family Favorites and Top of the Pops.
And those suits she wore back then,
they knocked off my naughty, nine-year-old socks.

And then I am back there in the swinging sixties,
with mania and miniskirts and boyhood fantasies.
Gone from hurricane, humid Houston
to stately, sensual Southern England,
immersed in glorious memories.
Roast lamb in the oven, we're back from church,
her voice on the radio rings out with passion across the land:
You don't have to say you love me, just be close at hand.

A feast of color greets us

CORAL STRAND

The labyrinth of twisting country roads delivers us finally
to the majestic coral shoreline.
A feast of color greets us:
magnificent blues from above shine down on soft white sands,
an array of green plants and dark seaweed adorns stones and shells,
all are perfectly disorganized along the shore to grace our sight.
A symphony of gulls cry-out their welcome,
as we walk across pebbles on down to the beach.
Pools of turquoise water sit serene between strands of rock,
which look out over the surrounding beauty like admiring statues.
We amble to the sea on crooked sandy paths,
basking in the early morning freshness,
the sun kindly warming our faces.
Faint white traces of cumulus clouds are littered in the otherwise perfect dawn sky.
The winds blow melodious over the rolling rhythm of the waves,
as they reach a crescendo and fall to the sand.
We brace ourselves as the cold water soaks our feet
and stand radiant feeling the fragrant sea air on our faces.
The memory of this glorious place will remain with us through time,
a perfect vision, reminding us of the splendor of creation.
All is well in our world, here in this time, here in this place.

Hibiscus rose and tall crepe myrtle, proud in pink the welcome throng

THE YARD

When the world is at me yelling, my head's abrim with stress and pain,
when it seems that all is lost and nothing may be gained,
I close the door and take my leave,
and sit out in the yard.

When I paint and colors run and my poetry won't rhyme,
when I dance and miss a beat or step on someone's pretty feet,
when it seems my world is incomplete,
I step outside into the yard.

When I call and knock and no one's home,
when I'm a warrior it seems and all alone,
I sound the retreat get off my throne,
and go hide out in the yard.

Hibiscus rose and tall crepe myrtle, proud in pink the welcome throng,
bring my mind back to a simple world, with nature's silent, soothing song
I hear the music, smell the roses,
out in the refuge of the yard.

And when the morning's fresh with fall, but your warmth is all I'm feeling,
we have our coffee and our books, everything we need for healing,
the patio's adorned with leaves and I know you're close to me,
we share the quiet and the glory,
we find our bliss out in the yard.

Here in the glory and quiet of nature

Desert in Bloom by Gabrielle Conway

NAMASTE

There is softness in the smile
and warmth in the wave.
I care about you fellow being
is what they are really trying to say.
The divine in me recognizes the divine in you
we are together, we are the same.
So then let our oneness flow.
Namaste

Here in the glory and quiet of nature
there in the manic city
replete with its passion, power, poverty and pity.
In our songs, our salutations, when we laugh and when we pray
goodwill towards others
is the order of the day.
Namaste

My look, my nod, my gesture and demeanor,
I am a fountain, a fable, maybe a dreamer.
I am sending you blessings from my spirit to yours
my energy I share, it's coming your way.
I send you peace, I send you joy and love
and what I truly want to say
is that I embrace your light and your divinity
and I am sending you mine.
Namaste

Wherever the moon may be, when sending its sustaining light

THE MOON IN GEMINI

Humid Houston with wine and hibiscus on a hot August night
The moon is in Gemini a waxing crescent
it shines down for us close and bright
Charming, witty, spontaneous and versatile
may we all be fun-loving Geminis
if just for a little while
We may relax and make merry
let go and rejoice
howl out dirges and praises
get on beat find our voice

But then what of tomorrow?
For there are only so many moons
to glow for us here on this earth
so why not have nights forever filled with Gemini spirit
that Gemini mirth
For wherever the moon may be
when sending its sustaining light
we can seize the day and dance by night
and claim freedom of spirit
as our given right

DEREK PICKETT * BIO

Derek Pickett was born and raised in the village of Hurstpierpoint in the English county of Sussex, where he grew up roving and roaming the green hills of the Sussex Downs, listening to as many records as he could get his hands on, and generally letting his imagination run free. It ran to Phoenix, Arizona one day and took him with it; and from there to San Francisco, Honolulu, Seattle, Mexico City, New York City and finally, to Houston, Texas, where he now lays his hat and which he now calls home.

He feels the rhythm of his life the most in his feet, and anybody who knows Derek will tell you that he's always dancing. And when he's not dancing, he's writing about dancing. The dance floor is where he both loses himself and finds himself.

He hopes that you enjoy this collection, and that you find or lose yourself on a dance floor somewhere soon.

—John-Paul Conway

www.ingramcontent.com/pod-product-compliance
Ingram Content Group UK Ltd.
Pitfield, Milton Keynes, MK11 3LW, UK
UKHW061203180426
11947UKWH00031B/2068